A Day at the Petting Zoo

FIRST EDITION
Series Editor Deborah Lock, Penny Smith; **Art Editor** Jacqueline Gooden;
US Editors Elizabeth Hester, John Searcy; **Production** Alison Lenane; **DTP Designer** Almudena Díaz;
Jacket Designer Hedi Gutt; **Reading Consultant** Linda Gambrell, PhD

THIS EDITION
Editorial Management by Oriel Square
Produced for DK by WonderLab Group LLC
Jennifer Emmett, Erica Green, Kate Hale, *Founders*

Editors Grace Hill Smith, Libby Romero, Michaela Weglinski;
Photography Editors Kelley Miller, Annette Kiesow, Nicole DiMella;
Managing Editor Rachel Houghton; **Designers** Project Design Company;
Researcher Michelle Harris; **Copy Editor** Lori Merritt; **Indexer** Connie Binder; **Proofreader** Larry Shea;
Reading Specialist Dr. Jennifer Albro; **Curriculum Specialist** Elaine Larson

---

Published in the United States by DK Publishing
1745 Broadway, 20th Floor, New York, NY 10019

Copyright © 2023 Dorling Kindersley Limited
DK, a Division of Penguin Random House LLC
23 24 25 26 27 10 9 8 7 6 5 4 3 2 1
001–333449–Apr/2023

All rights reserved.
Without limiting the rights under the copyright reserved
above, no part of this publication may be reproduced, stored
in or introduced into a retrieval system, or transmitted, in any
form, or by any means (electronic, mechanical, photocopying,
recording, or otherwise), without the prior written permission
of the copyright owner.
Published in Great Britain by Dorling Kindersley Limited

A catalog record for this book
is available from the Library of Congress.
HC ISBN: 978-0-7440-6769-9
PB ISBN: 978-0-7440-6770-5

DK books are available at special discounts when purchased
in bulk for sales promotions, premiums, fundraising, or
educational use. For details, contact: DK Publishing Special Markets,
1745 Broadway, 20th Floor, New York, NY 10019
SpecialSales@dk.com

Printed and bound in China

The publisher would like to thank the following for their kind permission to reproduce their images:
a=above; c=center; b=below; l=left; r=right; t=top; b/g=background
Dreamstime.com: Adogslifephoto 8bl; **Fotolia:** Anatolii 13br; **Shutterstock.com:** Blur Life 1975 16c, narikan 15c,
Hayk_Shalunts 26c, shupian 30, Studio 11 20c
Cover images: *Front:* **Dreamstime.com:** Blue Ring Education Pte Ltd (grass), Arif Budiyana (clouds),
Evgenii Naumov (fences); **Shutterstock.com:** Rita_Kochmarjova b; *Back:* **Dreamstime.com:** Gunel Abbasova clb,
Colorfuelstudio cra, Pavel Naumov cla; *Spine:* **Shutterstock.com:** Rita_Kochmarjova
All other images © Dorling Kindersley

For the curious
www.dk.com

A Day at the Petting Zoo

We are at the petting zoo.

We are petting a donkey.

 **donkeys**

ear

hoof

We are walking two baby llamas.

llamas

leash

I am brushing a pony.

ponies and horses

mane

pigs and piglets

hen

chicks

I am holding
a soft yellow chick.

chick

I am carrying
a green stick insect.

stick insects

frogs

I am watching a beady-eyed frog.

Ribbit! Ribbit!

toe

It is mealtime now.
I am giving the
woolly lamb some milk.

 **lambs**

wool

rabbits

I am feeding a hungry rabbit.

ear

carrot

This fluffy guinea pig is eating a leaf.

 **guinea pigs**

whiskers

claws

The white goose wants a snack.

geese

feathers

bill

goats

This long-horned goat is eating his lunch.

horn

Goodbye, animals!
It is time to go home.

Glossary

donkey
a small horse-like animal with long ears

frog
a short animal with long back legs

goose
a large bird with a long neck and a bill

llama
a large, woolly animal from South America

stick insect
a long, thin insect that looks like a stick

Quiz

Answer the questions to see what you have learned. Check your answers with an adult.

Which animal am I?

1. I am a fluffy animal with a long neck and pointed ears.
2. I am a pink animal with hooves and a snout.
3. I am a woolly baby sheep.
4. I am a bird with a long neck and a bill.
5. I have long horns and big, floppy ears.

1. A llama 2. A pig 3. A lamb 4. A goose 5. A long-horned goat